SCHOLASTIC

Skill-Building Math Activities
Kids Can't Resist!

by MICHELLE K. RAMSEY

New York • Toronto • London • Auckland • Sydney
Mexico City • New Delhi • Hong Kong • Buenos Aires

Teaching *Resources*

To my husband and boys: Bill, Billy, Blake, and Brady
Thanks for supporting me in all of my endeavors!

To my mom: Christina
Your faith and belief in me have inspired me to be the wife,
mother, and educator I am today.

Edited and produced by Immacula A. Rhodes
Cover design by Maria Lilja
Cover illustrations by Rusty Fletcher
Interior design by Holly Grundon
Interior illustrations by Rusty Fletcher, James Graham Hale, and Maxie Chambliss

ISBN-13: 978-0-439-57406-8
ISBN-10: 0-439-57406-4

Contents

Introduction

Skill-Building Math Activities Kids Can't Resist! provides a variety of fun and engaging activities, games, and manipulatives that can be used to teach and reinforce math skills kids need to know. Games and activities such as Hoppin' Addition Facts, Pizza Topping Patterns, and Money Bags help you address the needs and various learning styles of children while allowing them to experience success in math. In addition, all the activities correlate with the standards outlined by the National Council of Teachers of Mathematics (NCTM) in *Principles and Standards for School Mathematics* (2000).

Young children often find it difficult to sit still for long periods of time to complete worksheets. That's why I develop motivating activities that keep children actively engaged in learning. As I create, I focus on incorporating hands-on, fun, and out-of-the-ordinary elements in my games and activities. Often, I seek new ideas and ways to convert the "in" craze or unusual things into teaching games. I've learned over the years that activities which include high-interest materials and formats help children develop a positive attitude toward learning and make learning more meaningful and fun.

You can use the games, manipulatives, and activities that I present in this book in a variety of ways. From individual assessment to large group participation, the activities help provide positive motivation for children to achieve. Also, you can incorporate different skills into many of the game formats, allowing you to use the learning games throughout the year with little additional time or effort. Whether you want children to practice addition skills, create patterns, or learn about time and money concepts, you'll find a fun activity in *Skill-Building Math Activities Kids Can't Resist!* that fits the need. Enjoy!

—Michelle K. Ramsey

How to Use This Book

The activities and games in *Skill-Building Math Activities Kids Can't Resist!* were designed to help you engage children in active ways to practice and master essential math skills. Here's an overview of what you'll find on each activity page:

Skill

As a quick reference, the targeted math skill is shown at the top of each activity page.

Players

Look here to find out how many children can participate in the activity or game.

Materials

In this section, you'll find a list of materials needed to prepare and use the activity. Most of the materials include basic art supplies that can be found right in your classroom, such as crayons, scissors, glue, and construction paper. Other materials are usually readily available or easy to gather and prepare. For activities that call for one or more dice, you can use standard dice. If desired, you can convert the dice to number cubes simply by placing a dot sticker on each side and writing the number for that side on the sticker. If the activity requires one or more reproducible patterns, you can check this list to find the specific pattern needed and the page on which it is found.

Getting Ready

The step-by-step directions in this section tell you how to prepare and set up the materials for the activity or game. To make sturdier game boards and cards, you might want to copy the patterns directly onto tagboard or mount them on construction paper. Often, laminating the game pieces is suggested to make them more durable. When the materials for an activity are not in use, you might store them in a resealable plastic bag labeled with the activity name.

How to Play

Check this section for directions on how to use the activity or play the game. To introduce the activity or game, you can participate in it for the first round or assist children as they play. If a game requires turn taking, help children come up with a method for determining the order in which players will take turns. For example, they can roll a die, draw a number, or take turns in the order of their birthdays.

Variations

Use the ideas here to challenge or extend children's learning. These suggestions provide additional practice in the targeted skill or give ideas on how to adapt the activity or materials to reinforce other essential math skills.

On page 8, you'll find a matrix that identifies the primary skills covered by each activity in this book. You can use this handy reference as a guide in choosing activities that address a particular topic, a curriculum focal point, or a skill that connects to a focal point. To learn more about the NCTM standards, visit **www.nctm.org/ standards**.

Connections With the NCTM Skills Standards

Each activity in *Skill-Building Math Activities Kids Can't Resist!* focuses on a specific skill that correlates with one of the following NCTM standards for content and processes: number and operations; patterns, functions, and algebra; geometry and spatial sense; measurement; and data analysis, statistics, and probability. In addition to these standards, the NCTM has identified three curriculum focal points for each grade level, PreK–8. These focal points, or areas of content emphasis, form the foundation of mathematical learning. They include concepts or topics that are useful both in and outside of school and connect with the math learned in earlier and later grades. The curriculum focal points for each grade level addressed in this book are:

Kindergarten—Number and Operations; Geometry; Measurement

Grade 1—Number and Operations; Algebra; Geometry

Grade 2—Number and Operations; Algebra; Measurement

Helpful Hints

The following hints are provided to help you incorporate the games and activities into your classroom routine. Remember that math should be taught and reinforced on a daily basis. What better way than to provide children with a variety of hands-on games and activities!

- Establish a designated area in your classroom as a math learning center. Purchase a large pegboard to mount on a wall in the center. Also, purchase peg hooks and rings to use on the pegboard. You can punch holes in all your flash cards, game boards, and other materials to hang on the board. Game pieces and smaller items can be kept in small plastic baskets that have been hung on the hooks. With all your math activities and games conveniently located in one place, children can easily access the materials for independent work or center time.

- The plastic rings used for six-pack canned drinks can be used to create another way to display game boards and materials. Use yarn to tie the plastic rings together to form a large sheet of rings. Hang the sheet in your center and clip game boards and other materials to it with clothespins.

- Purchase a plastic chain that has large plastic clips attached to it. Hang the chain in your center and clip on games and activities.

- Make a set of flash cards for addition and subtraction math facts up to 18. Divide each set into two difficulty levels (facts from 1 to 9 might be level 1, and facts from 10 to 18 level 2). Place the number corresponding to the level of each math fact on the back of the card. Children can use the different levels of cards according to their ability and learning needs.

- If you want to introduce or review an activity with the whole class, you can make a transparency of the corresponding reproducible patterns (such as recording sheets and cards). Then display the transparencies on an overhead projector to demonstrate to children how to use the materials.

- To make the games more attractive and appealing, decorate the game boards with stickers, cut the edges of game pieces with decorative shape-scissors, or glue the game boards on colored construction paper or file folders.

- The games and activities provided can be used with individuals, small groups, or large groups. Many of them can be used for assessment. For example, a child can play a game or participate in an activity while you observe and assess what the child knows. Most important, choose activities that reflect your instructional goals, meet each child's needs, and make learning fun. Enjoy!

Extending Learning

There are many ways to extend children's learning—both in and out of the classroom. Call children's attention to math concepts throughout the day and in any setting. For example, while at recess, point out the different shapes found on the playground equipment. Or ask children to compare the number of people seated at different tables in the cafeteria. Look for opportunities to incorporate math while teaching other subject areas as well. And be sure to encourage children to look for ways to use their math skills at home and during after-school activities.

Home-School Connections

A child's home environment is important to the success a child experiences in school. Parents and family members can be some of the greatest assets in ensuring that a child has the math background to succeed. There are three main ways to help make strong home-school connections using the games and activities presented in this book.

1. Conduct a parent make-and-take workshop. During the workshop, present the different activities parents can use to reinforce the skills you are teaching. Provide time for parents to laminate the games they make. Children can also participate in the workshop.

2. During the week, have each child make a game or activity to take home. Provide a step-by-step demonstration. Then allow children to create the games during independent or center time.

3. Make additional games and activities to send home with children (you might solicit the help of parent volunteers). Or invite parents to check out games from your classroom to use at home with their child.

Remember, the games and activities you send home should be an extension of the day's activities. Send home only games that reinforce the skills a child needs. Be sure to include simple activity instructions with each game.

Additional Ideas

Here are more ideas to motivate and keep children learning. You can use these in the classroom, or prepare the materials to send home.

Mystery Operations: Divide a 9-inch circle into eight sections. Write an addition or subtraction fact in each section near the rim, omitting the operation sign (for example, 4 __ 5 = 9). Label the closed end of eight clothespins with plus (+) and eight more with minus (–). To use, children clip a clothespin to each problem to fill in the missing sign.

Soupy Shapes: Cut out and laminate different shapes in various sizes. Put all the shapes in a pot. Invite children to spoon out as many shapes at a time as possible and then name each shape. They might also remove shapes and order them by size or use them to create patterns.

Connections With the NCTM Standards

Connections With the NCTM Standards 2000	Number and Operations	Estimation *	Number Sense and Numeration *	Concepts of Whole-Number Operations *	Whole-Number Computations *	Fractions and Decimals *	Patterns, Functions, and Algebra	Geometry and Spatial Sense	Measurement	Data Analysis, Statistics, and Probability	Problem Solving	Reasoning and Proof	Communication	Connections	Representation
Flippin' Number Lids	X		X				X				X	X	X	X	X
Skip-Counting Cards	X		X				X				X	X	X	X	X
Duckling Number Comparisons	X		X								X	X	X	X	X
Place-Value Fly Swat	X		X	X	X		X				X	X	X	X	X
Addition Bat	X		X	X	X		X				X	X	X	X	X
Hoppin' Addition Facts	X		X	X	X						X	X	X	X	X
Mystery Addends	X		X	X	X		X				X	X	X	X	X
Musical Subtraction Facts	X		X	X	X						X	X	X	X	X
Math Fact Flowers	X		X	X	X						X	X	X	X	X
Alphabet Addition	X		X	X	X		X				X	X	X	X	X
Wipe-Off Shape Pads	X		X				X	X			X	X	X	X	X
Pizza Topping Patterns	X		X	X	X		X	X			X	X	X	X	X
Apple Number Patterns	X		X	X	X		X				X	X	X	X	X
Shop-and-Sort	X		X	X	X		X			X	X	X	X	X	X
Egg-Carton Probability	X		X							X	X	X	X	X	X
Scoop-and-Estimate	X	X	X							X	X	X	X	X	X
Data Collector Chart	X		X	X	X					X	X	X	X	X	X
Tick-Tock Lid Clock	X		X						X		X	X	X	X	X
Money Bags	X		X	X	X						X	X	X	X	X
Inchworm Measurements	X		X						X		X	X	X	X	X
Temperature Zip	X		X						X	X	X	X	X	X	X
Gallon Guy	X		X						X		X	X	X	X	X
Word Problem Spin	X		X	X	X					X	X	X	X	X	X

*Indicates a subcategory of Number and Operations

Flippin' Number Lids

Children practice one-to-one correspondence with numbered milk jug lids.

Players: 2

Materials

- 100 clean, plastic milk jug lids
- 100 same-colored dot stickers (1 ¼-inch works well)
- fine-tip permanent marker
- 22- by 28-inch posterboard
- ruler

Getting Ready

1. Stick a dot sticker on the flat side of each milk jug lid.

2. Write a different number from 1 to 100 on the sticker on each lid.

3. Use the ruler and marker to draw a 100-box grid on the posterboard, making each box a 2-inch square.

How to Play

1. Players work together to sequence the lids, numbers faceup, on the grid. Then they count the lids from 1 to 100.

2. The first player covers his or her eyes while the second player flips five lids upside down on the grid.

3. The second player decides which number belongs in each box with an upside-down lid. He or she names the missing number and then flips that lid to check the answer.

4. The players switch roles for the next round of play.

Variations

- To practice recognizing numbers, call out numbers and have children point out the corresponding lids.
- Ask a child to give his or her partner two lids from the grid to compare. Have the partner tell which of the numbers is the larger (or smaller) of the two and then check his or her answer by placing the lids in their corresponding boxes on the grid.

Skip-Counting Cards

Children use picture cards to practice skip counting by 2s, 3s, 4s, and 5s.

Players: 2

Materials

- skip-counting cards (pages 11–13)
- color markers
- scissors
- pair of dice
- wipe-off markers (one per player)
- paper towels

Getting Ready

1. Make two copies of each set of skip-counting cards. Color, laminate, and cut apart the cards.

2. Explain which skip-counting increment will be used with each type of card: 2 for the two wheels on the bike; 3 for the three snowballs on the snowman; 4 for the four leaves on the clover; and 5 for the five fingers on the handprint.

How to Play

1. Sort and stack each set of cards faceup.

2. The first player rolls a die as many times as needed until it lands on 2, 3, 4, or 5. He or she will use the cards corresponding to that number increment.

3. The player rolls the pair of dice and takes that many cards from the appropriate stack.

4. The player lines up and skip-counts the cards by the appropriate increment. Then he or she writes the corresponding number on each card in the sequence.

5. Both players check the numbers for correctness. Then the first player erases the cards and returns them to the stack.

6. Players switch roles and play again, continuing until each player has had five turns.

Variations

- To make the activity more challenging, use three or more sets of each kind of card and the same number of dice. For example, if children use four dice, they'll need four sets of cards.
- Invite pairs to practice patterning with the cards. Ask one child to create a pattern with the cards, such as bike, clover, hand, bike, clover, hand. Have his or her partner duplicate the pattern.

Skip-Counting Cards

Skill-Building Math Activities Kids Can't Resist! © 2007 by Michelle K. Ramsey, Scholastic Teaching Resources

Skip-Counting Cards

Skip-Counting Cards

Skill-Building Math Activities Kids Can't Resist! © 2007 by Michelle K. Ramsey, Scholastic Teaching Resources

Duckling Number Comparisons

Children compare numbers using these delightful ducklings.

Players: 2

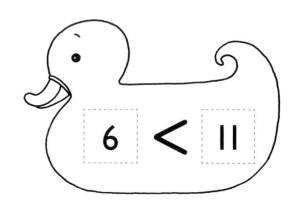

Materials

- duckling patterns and number cards (pages 15–16)
- yellow construction paper (optional)
- color markers
- scissors

Getting Ready

1. Copy the duckling patterns and number cards.

2. Color the duckling patterns. (If desired, copy the patterns on yellow paper.)

3. Laminate and cut out the duckling patterns and number cards.

How to Play

1. Shuffle the number cards and stack them facedown.

2. Each player takes one duckling.

3. Each player draws a card and places it on either square on his or her duckling.

4. Each player draws another card. If the player can place the card on his or her duckling and the number comparison works, the player earns a point. If not, the player does not earn a point.

5. Players return their cards to the bottom of the stack and play again. The first player to earn five points wins the game.

Variations

- Have younger children practice one-to-one correspondence and counting by using manipulatives to count and check their work.

- For individual practice, ask children to choose two cards at a time and place them on either of the ducklings to make a correct number comparison sentence. Have children continue until they have made ten number comparisons or used all the cards. Encourage them to alternate using the ducklings so they can practice comparing numbers with each sign.

Duckling Number Comparisons

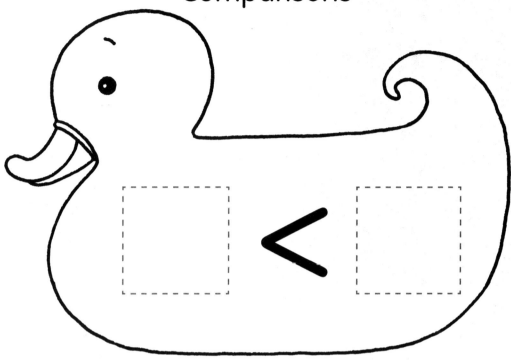

Duckling Number Comparisons

Duckling Number Comparisons

0	1	2	3	4
5	6	7	8	9
10	11	12	13	14
15	16	17	18	19
20	21	22	23	24
25	26	27	28	29
30	31	32	33	34

Skill-Building Math Activities Kids Can't Resist! © 2007 by Michelle K. Ramsey, Scholastic Teaching Resources

Place-Value Fly Swat

Children swat number flies to demonstrate understanding of place value.

Players: whole class

Materials

- number fly cards (pages 18–19)
- color markers
- scissors
- chalkboard
- chalk
- chalkboard eraser
- new, unused fly swatters

Getting Ready

1. Color and laminate a copy of the fly cards. Cut the cards apart.

2. Tape the cards to the chalkboard, creating three rows of cards and putting them in any order you desire. Leave 4 to 6 inches between the cards. (Make sure the cards are within easy reach of children.)

How to Play

1. Divide the class into two teams. The first player on the first team takes the fly swatter and stands in front of the cards on the chalkboard.

2. In large writing, print a 2- or 3-digit number on the chalkboard off to the side of the cards. (Be sure not to repeat any digits in the number.) Have the player read the number aloud.

3. Decide which placeholder in the number, such as ones, tens, or hundreds, that you want the player to identify. Call out "Swat the ___!" filling in the blank with the placeholder. The player then swats the fly labeled with the number found in that position. If correct, the player earns a point for his or her team.

4. Erase the number and write a new one on the board for the first player on the second team. Play continues until each player has had a turn. The team with the most points at the end of the game is the winner.

Variation

Write simple addition equations with missing addends, from 0 to 9, on large index cards. To use, show players a card and have them swat the fly labeled with the number for the missing addend.

Number Fly Cards

18

Number Fly Cards

Addition Bat

Children practice basic addition facts with this adorable bat.

Players: 2

Materials

- bat head and wing patterns (page 21)
- crayons
- scissors
- black construction paper
- pencil
- wire clothes hanger
- craft glue
- plastic or wooden clothespins in two colors

Getting Ready

1. Make two copies of the bat head and wing patterns. Draw a face on one of the bat heads.

2. Color, cut out, and laminate the heads and wings.

3. Glue the back of the heads together, trapping the hanger hook between them.

4. Fold each wing in half. Glue a wing to each side of the hanger, fitting the fold over the slanted wire. (You might use clothespins to hold the pieces in place until the glue dries.)

How to Play

1. The first player clips from 1 to 9 same-colored clothespins to one side of the bottom of the bat. He or she clips 1 to 9 clothespins of a different color on the other side.

2. The second player adds the clothespins on each side of the bat. He or she tells the sum. The first player checks the answer by counting all the clothespins on the bat.

3. Players remove the clothespins and switch roles to play again.

Variations

- Reinforce addition facts for a given number. For example, for the 6 facts family, place 6 clothespins on the left side of the bat. Then place different quantities of clothespins on the right side and have children find the sums.
- Teach children about the commutative property of addition. First, use the two colors of clothespins to set up a problem on the bat. After the child finds the sum, flip the hanger over and have him or her solve the "new" problem. Explain that the answer is the same even though the addends have been reversed.

Addition Bat

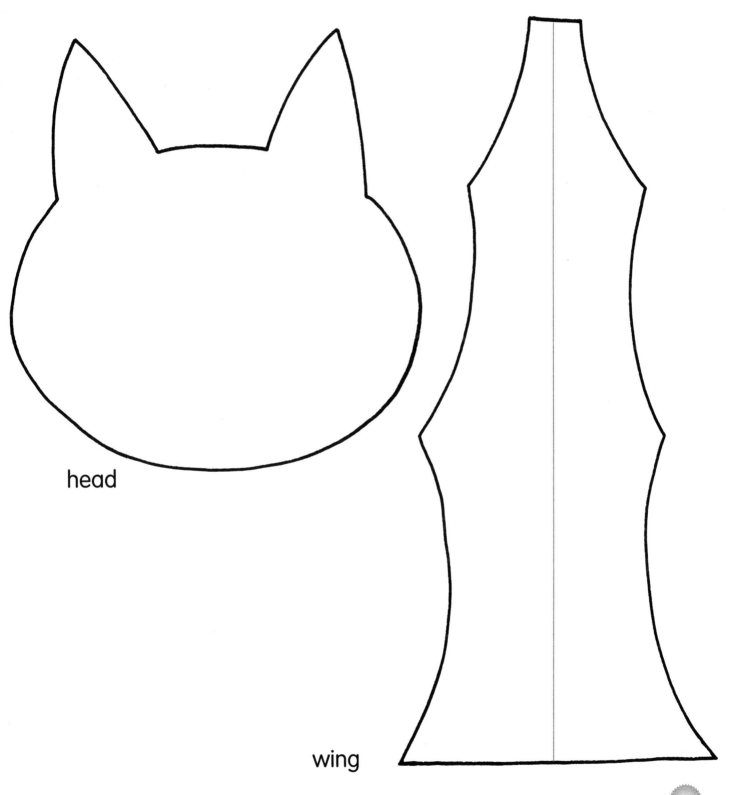

head

wing

Hoppin' Addition Facts

Children play hopscotch to practice basic addition facts.

Skill
addition
facts

Players: 2

Materials

- addition fact cards (pages 24–26)
- white vinyl shower curtain (extra long works well)
- permanent marker
- 10 index cards
- scissors
- paper lunch bag
- tape
- duct tape
- paper
- pencil

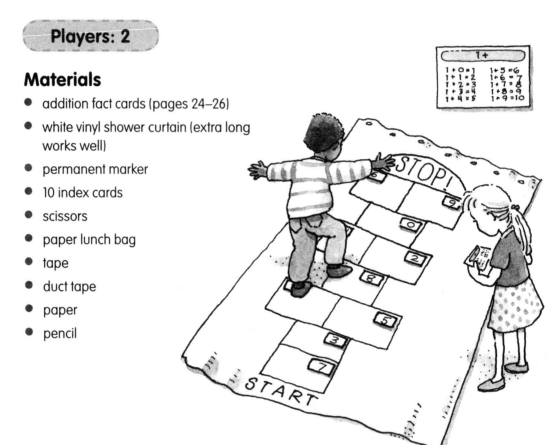

Getting Ready

1. Use the permanent marker to draw a hopscotch game board, with 9-inch squares on the shower curtain, as shown.

2. Write a different number from 0 to 9 on each index card.

3. Laminate the number cards and a copy of the addition fact cards. Then cut apart the fact cards and put them in the paper bag.

4. Tape a number card in the top corner of each hopscotch square between Start and Stop. Place the cards in any order you desire.

5. Spread out the hopscotch game board on the floor. Use duct tape at the corners to hold it in place.

How to Play

1. One player takes the role of the hopper and the other player is the caller. The caller takes the pencil and paper.

2. The hopper draws a fact card from the bag and hands it to the caller. The caller reads the boldfaced number and symbol at the top of the card, such as "8 +." This will be the number the hopper adds to other numbers during his or her turn.

3. Beginning at Start, the hopper hops onto one block of the hopscotch game board at a time (he or she may stand in the block on one or both feet). Each time, he or she creates an addition problem using the number and symbol from the fact card and the number on the hopscotch block (for example 8 + 7). Then the hopper gives the sum.

4. The caller checks the fact card to see if the hopper gave the correct answer. If correct, the caller writes down one point for the hopper.

5. The hopper continues until he or she reaches Stop. Then the players switch roles and play again.

6. The player with the most points after five rounds is the winner.

Variations

- Prepare and use the subtraction fact cards in the game. For this version, the hopper subtracts the number on each hopscotch block from the number at the top of the subtraction fact card.
- To practice 3-digit addition, invite children to toss three beanbags onto the hopscotch blocks. Have them add the three numbers on which the bags land.

Addition Fact Cards

1 +

1 + 0 = 1	1 + 5 = 6
1 + 1 = 2	1 + 6 = 7
1 + 2 = 3	1 + 7 = 8
1 + 3 = 4	1 + 8 = 9
1 + 4 = 5	1 + 9 = 10

2 +

2 + 0 = 2	2 + 5 = 7
2 + 1 = 3	2 + 6 = 8
2 + 2 = 4	2 + 7 = 9
2 + 3 = 5	2 + 8 = 10
2 + 4 = 6	2 + 9 = 11

3 +

3 + 0 = 3	3 + 5 = 8
3 + 1 = 4	3 + 6 = 9
3 + 2 = 5	3 + 7 = 10
3 + 3 = 6	3 + 8 = 11
3 + 4 = 7	3 + 9 = 12

4 +

4 + 0 = 4	4 + 5 = 9
4 + 1 = 5	4 + 6 = 10
4 + 2 = 6	4 + 7 = 11
4 + 3 = 7	4 + 8 = 12
4 + 4 = 8	4 + 9 = 13

5 +

5 + 0 = 5	5 + 5 = 10
5 + 1 = 6	5 + 6 = 11
5 + 2 = 7	5 + 7 = 12
5 + 3 = 8	5 + 8 = 13
5 + 4 = 9	5 + 9 = 14

6 +

6 + 0 = 6	6 + 5 = 11
6 + 1 = 7	6 + 6 = 12
6 + 2 = 8	6 + 7 = 13
6 + 3 = 9	6 + 8 = 14
6 + 4 = 10	6 + 9 = 15

Addition and Subtraction Fact Cards

7 +

7 + 0 = 7	7 + 5 = 12
7 + 1 = 8	7 + 6 = 13
7 + 2 = 9	7 + 7 = 14
7 + 3 = 10	7 + 8 = 15
7 + 4 = 11	7 + 9 = 16

8 +

8 + 0 = 8	8 + 5 = 13
8 + 1 = 9	8 + 6 = 14
8 + 2 = 10	8 + 7 = 15
8 + 3 = 11	8 + 8 = 16
8 + 4 = 12	8 + 9 = 17

9 +

9 + 0 = 9	9 + 5 = 14
9 + 1 = 10	9 + 6 = 15
9 + 2 = 11	9 + 7 = 16
9 + 3 = 12	9 + 8 = 17
9 + 4 = 13	9 + 9 = 18

10 −

10 − 0 = 10	10 − 5 = 5
10 − 1 = 9	10 − 6 = 4
10 − 2 = 8	10 − 7 = 3
10 − 3 = 7	10 − 8 = 2
10 − 4 = 6	10 − 9 = 1

11 −

11 − 0 = 11	11 − 5 = 6
11 − 1 = 10	11 − 6 = 5
11 − 2 = 9	11 − 7 = 4
11 − 3 = 8	11 − 8 = 3
11 − 4 = 7	11 − 9 = 2

12 −

12 − 0 = 12	12 − 5 = 7
12 − 1 = 11	12 − 6 = 6
12 − 2 = 10	12 − 7 = 5
12 − 3 = 9	12 − 8 = 4
12 − 4 = 8	12 − 9 = 3

Skill-Building Math Activities Kids Can't Resist! © 2007 by Michelle K. Ramsey, Scholastic Teaching Resources

Subtraction Fact Cards

13 –

13 – 0 = 13	13 – 5 = 8
13 – 1 = 12	13 – 6 = 7
13 – 2 = 11	13 – 7 = 6
13 – 3 = 10	13 – 8 = 5
13 – 4 = 9	13 – 9 = 4

14 –

14 – 0 = 14	14 – 5 = 9
14 – 1 = 13	14 – 6 = 8
14 – 2 = 12	14 – 7 = 7
14 – 3 = 11	14 – 8 = 6
14 – 4 = 10	14 – 9 = 5

15 –

15 – 0 = 15	15 – 5 = 10
15 – 1 = 14	15 – 6 = 9
15 – 2 = 13	15 – 7 = 8
15 – 3 = 12	15 – 8 = 7
15 – 4 = 11	15 – 9 = 6

16 –

16 – 0 = 16	16 – 5 = 11
16 – 1 = 15	16 – 6 = 10
16 – 2 = 14	16 – 7 = 9
16 – 3 = 13	16 – 8 = 8
16 – 4 = 12	16 – 9 = 7

17 –

17 – 0 = 17	17 – 5 = 12
17 – 1 = 16	17 – 6 = 11
17 – 2 = 15	17 – 7 = 10
17 – 3 = 14	17 – 8 = 9
17 – 4 = 13	17 – 9 = 8

18 –

18 – 0 = 18	18 – 5 = 13
18 – 1 = 17	18 – 6 = 12
18 – 2 = 16	18 – 7 = 11
18 – 3 = 15	18 – 8 = 10
18 – 4 = 14	18 – 9 = 9

Mystery Addends

Children practice basic addition facts by finding the mystery addends.

Players: 3

Materials

- 20 plain index cards
- black permanent marker

Getting Ready

1. Write 0 to 9 on index cards two times, creating two cards for each number.

2. Laminate the number cards for durability.

The sum of the numbers is 11!

How to Play

1. Shuffle the cards and place the stack facedown. Then choose a player to be the caller.

2. The other two players each take a card from the stack without looking at the number. Each player places the card against his or her forehead with the number facing out. The caller and other player should be able to see the number on the card, but the cardholder should not be able to see his or her own card.

3. The caller mentally adds the two numbers and calls out the sum. For example, if one player is holding 6 and the other 5, the caller will call out 11. The cardholders look at each other's cards. They use that number and the sum provided by the caller to try to determine the mystery addend—that is, the number card they are holding.

4. Each cardholder tells what number he or she thinks is the mystery addend. Then the cardholders look at their own cards to check their answers.

5. Continue play until all the cards have been used. Then have players switch roles and play again.

Variation

To reinforce number sequencing skills, ask the caller to name the number that comes before and after each cardholder's number. Have the cardholder use the information to determine what number is on his or her card.

Musical Subtraction Facts

Use this musical game to give children practice in subtraction facts.

Players: 18

Materials

- 9 half-sheets of construction paper for each subtraction fact family (use a different color for each fact family)
- black permanent marker
- 9 quart-sized resealable plastic bags
- record player or CD player
- lively music

Getting Ready

1. Choose a subtraction fact family. Write a different fact from that family on each of the nine half-sheets in a color set. Create a set for each fact family.

2. Puzzle-cut each page between the subtrahend and equal sign to create a two-piece puzzle. Laminate all the puzzle pieces.

3. Store each set of fact family puzzles in a separate resealable plastic bag. Label the bag with the fact family.

How to Play

1. Choose a set of subtraction fact puzzles. Form a large circle on the floor with the puzzle pieces, placing each piece facedown.

2. Each child stands beside a puzzle piece on the outside of the circle.

3. Children walk around the circle as music is played. When the music stops, each child stops, picks up the nearest puzzle piece, and turns it over.

4. Children work together to try to match all the puzzle pieces. When a child finds his or her puzzle partner, the pair sits down.

5. After children are seated with their partners, the pairs take turns standing and reading their subtraction facts to the group.

Variation

Invite children to use the puzzles for individual practice. They can self-check their work by making sure the pieces of each puzzle fit together properly.

Math Fact Flowers

Children use self-checking flowers to practice addition and subtraction facts.

Players: 2

Materials

- flower pattern (page 30)
- 18 sheets of light-colored construction paper (optional)
- crayons
- scissors
- black permanent marker

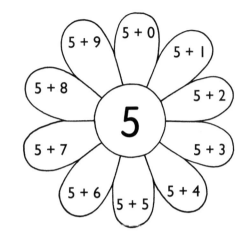

Getting Ready

1. Make 18 copies of the flower pattern. Color and cut out each flower. (Rather than coloring the flowers, you might copy the pattern on light-colored construction paper.)

2. Use the permanent marker to write a number from 1 to 9 in the center of each flower. Use each number on two flowers. On one flower in each number pair, write an addition fact on each petal using the number in the center and a number from 0 to 9. Similarly, write subtraction facts on the other flower in the pair.

3. Fold each petal in and write the answer on the back. It is helpful to write the whole math sentence (for example, 4 + 0 = 4).

4. Laminate the flowers for durability.

How to Play

1. Each player chooses a flower.

2. Players take turns choosing a petal on their flower and saying the problem aloud. Each player folds the corresponding petal in to check the answer on the back. If correct, the player earns one point.

3. Players continue the game until they have answered all the problems on the flowers. The player with the most points wins that round.

Variation

To make math fact flowers for mixed review, leave the center of each flower blank. Write addition and subtraction problems belonging to different fact families on the petals.

Flower Pattern

Alphabet Addition

Children use an alphabetical number key to create 1- and 2-digit problems to solve.

Skill

1- and 2-digit addition

Players: 2

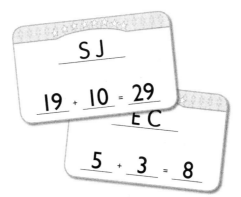

Materials

- letter-number key (page 32)
- equation cards (page 33)
- wipe-off markers (one per player)
- paper towels

Letter-Number Key

A	B	C	D	E
1	2	3	4	5
F	G	H	I	J
6	7	8	9	10
K	L	M	N	O
11	12	13	14	15
P	Q	R	S	T
16	17	18	19	20
U	V	W	X	Y
21	22	23	24	25
Z				
26				

Getting Ready

1. Copy and laminate the letter-number key and two copies of the equation cards.

2. Cut apart the equation cards.

How to Play

1. Each player takes an equation card bordered with stars. The player writes his or her initials on the top line.

2. Each player uses the letter-number key to find the number corresponding to each letter in the initials on his or her card. He or she writes these numbers on the addend lines in the equation. Then the player solves the problem and writes the answer.

3. Players exchange cards and check each other's answers. Then they erase their cards and play again, using other classmates' initials or two-letter words, such as "be," "it," and "on."

4. To practice addition with three addends, children write three-letter words on the equation cards bordered with dots.

Variations

- Before erasing their equation cards, have children compare the answers on the two cards to decide which set of initials or word has the higher number value.
- Ask children to compare the values of the two letters in their initials or in a two-letter word. Have them subtract the lower value from the higher one.

Letter-Number Key

A	B	C	D	E
1	2	3	4	5
F	G	H	I	J
6	7	8	9	10
K	L	M	N	O
11	12	13	14	15
P	Q	R	S	T
16	17	18	19	20
U	V	W	X	Y
21	22	23	24	25
Z				
26				

Equation Cards

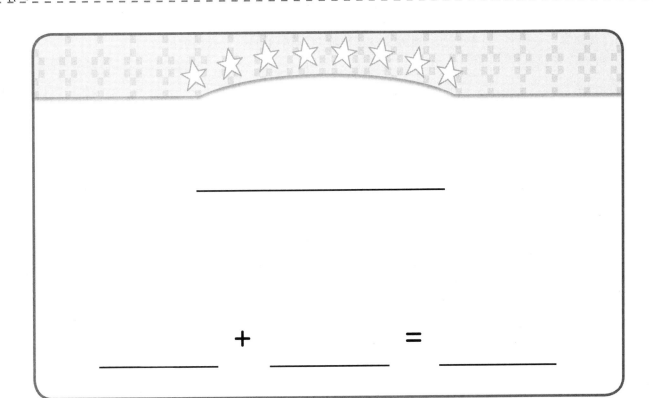

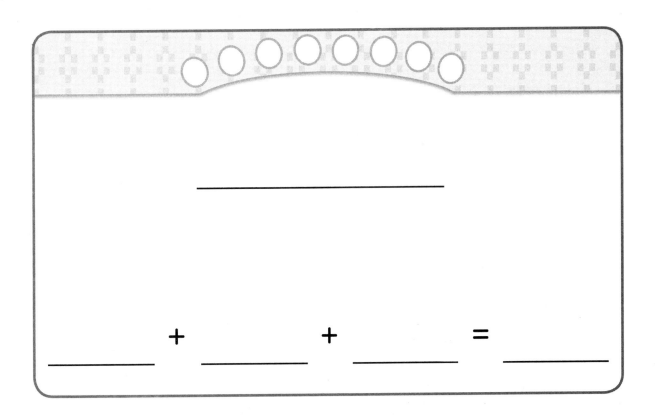

Wipe-Off Shape Pads

Children explore shape concepts with these inexpensive, easy-to-make work pads.

Skill
shape concepts

Players: 6

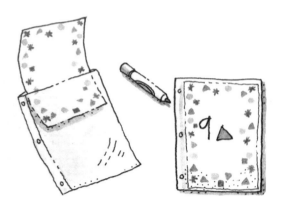

Materials

- six 8 ½- by 11-inch sheets of posterboard
- rubber shape stamps
- washable ink pads in different colors
- six 8 ½- by 11-inch clear page protectors
- wipe-off markers (one per player)
- paper towels

Getting Ready

1. Use the shape stamps and ink to create a border around each sheet of posterboard. You might stamp shapes at random or create a pattern with the shapes, using as many different shapes and colors as desired to create colorful, interesting borders. Make sure the shapes do not overlap.

2. Slip each posterboard into a separate page protector.

How to Play

1. Each player chooses a shape pad.

2. Name a shape, such as square, circle, or star. Players search their pads and count how many times that shape appears in the border. Then they use a wipe-off marker to write their findings and draw the given shape on their pad.

3. Players exchange shape pads and check each other's work.

4. Players erase their shape pads to prepare for the next round of play.

5. For each round, name a different shape for children to find and count.

Variation

Draw a line of shapes to create a pattern (such as square, circle, triangle, square, circle, triangle) across the top half of a sheet of paper. Draw other shape patterns on several more pages. Then slip each page into a separate page protector. Have children extend each pattern as far as possible by drawing the sequence of shapes on their pad.

Pizza Topping Patterns

Children create and duplicate patterns with pizza toppings.

Players: 2

Materials

- pizza patterns and pizza topping cards (pages 36–37)
- crayons
- scissors

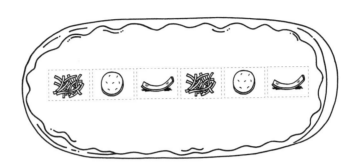

Getting Ready

1. Copy the pizza patterns and pizza topping cards. Color each pizza and topping a solid color. You might make several sets of the topping cards.

2. Laminate and cut out all the pieces.

3. Tell children which topping each card represents: pepperoni, mushroom, pepper, olive, and cheese.

How to Play

1. Each player takes a pizza.

2. The first player chooses two or three kinds of toppings. He or she uses the toppings to create a pattern on the pizza. Then the second player duplicates the pattern on his or her pizza.

3. As an alternative, each player begins a two- or three-topping pattern across the top of his or her pizza. Then the other player takes the pizza and extends the pattern with the appropriate toppings.

Variations

- Use the pizzas to practice simple word problems. Make up a word problem, such as "Sam's pizza was topped with 4 pepperoni and 3 olives. How many toppings were on his pizza?" Have children use the pizzas and toppings to solve the problem.
- Reinforce sorting and classifying skills. Ask children to sort the toppings by shape. Have them discuss how each topping shape differs from or is similar to the other shapes. Then challenge children to identify objects around the room that have the same shape as each topping.

Pizza Patterns

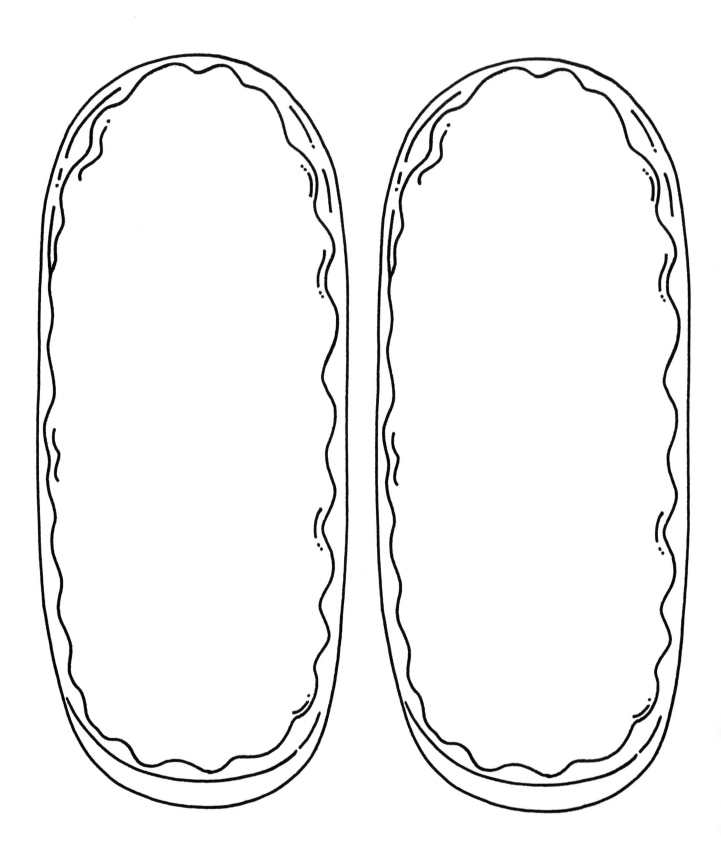

Pizza Topping Cards

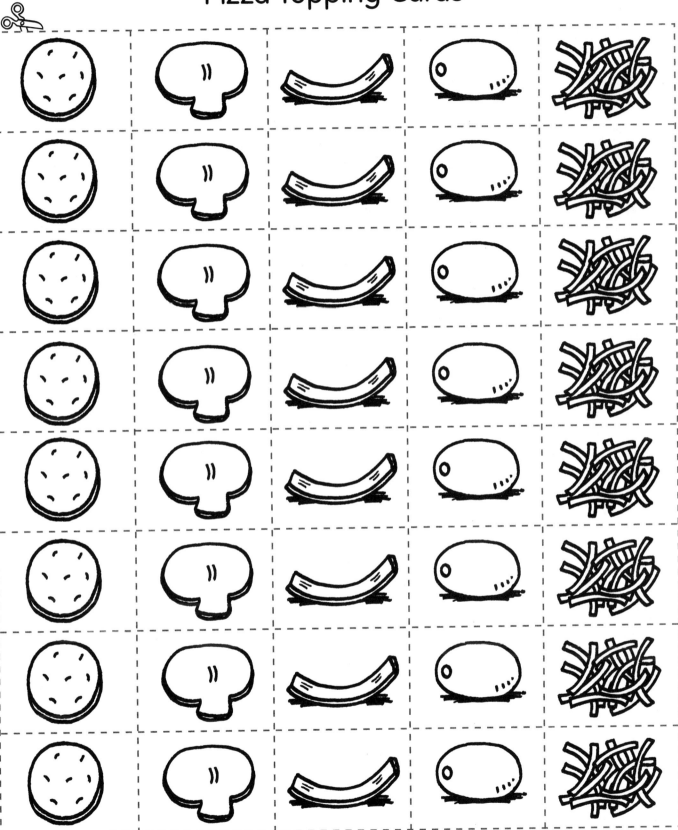

Apple Number Patterns

Children create number patterns with this basket full of apple delights.

Players: 2

Materials

- apple basket and cards (pages 39–40)
- crayons
- scissors
- wipe-off marker
- paper towels

Getting Ready

1. Copy and color the apple basket and cards (you might make several sets of the apple cards). Laminate and cut out all of the pieces.

2. Use the wipe-off marker to write a different number on each apple card. You can number the cards sequentially, starting with 1, or use the number range of your choice.

3. Explain that children will create a number pattern by adding or subtracting a specific number shown on the basket (you will write the number). For example, if "–2" is in the box, children will create a pattern by subtracting 2.

How to Play

1. Decide on the operation and increment to be used to create the number pattern. Use the wipe-off marker to write the corresponding symbol and number on the basket.

2. Choose an appropriate number card to use as the starter number for the pattern. Place the card in the top left corner of the basket.

3. Players work together to create a number pattern with the number cards, using the operation and increment shown on the basket.

4. When the basket is full, or all the possible cards have been used, players check their number pattern for correctness.

5. To play again, remove the cards, erase what's written in the box on the basket, and write in a new operation and increment. Then place an appropriate starter card on the tray.

Variation

Label the apple cards with an assortment of one-, two-, and three-digit numbers. Have children sort the cards by odd and even numbers. Or have them sort the cards by the place value held by a specific digit. For example, they might sort out all the cards with a 3 in the tens place.

Apple Basket

Apple Cards

  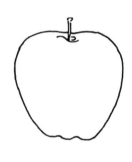 

 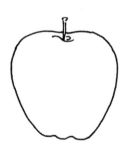  

Skill-Building Math Activities Kids Can't Resist! © 2007 by Michelle K. Ramsey, Scholastic Teaching Resources

Shop-and-Sort

Children sort and classify grocery items by food type and price.

Players: 2

Materials

- grocery store food ads
- large index cards
- scissors
- glue stick
- markers
- 2 plastic shopping baskets
- tape

Getting Ready

1. Cut out pictured food items from the grocery store ads. Glue each picture to an index card. Use pictures that fit into categories, such as canned, frozen, and fresh foods. Write the name of the item and its price under the picture. Laminate all the cards.

2. Write "99¢ and Lower" and "$1.00 and Higher" on separate index cards. Tape a card to each basket.

How to Play

1. Place the food cards faceup on the table. Assign each player a category, such as canned, fresh, or frozen foods.

2. Players look through the cards to find food items that belong to their assigned categories. When finished, players exchange their cards to check each other's work.

3. Using the cards for their assigned categories, players sort the foods by price, placing each card in the corresponding basket.

4. Each player chooses a basket and checks to make sure all the cards in the basket have been placed correctly.

5. For additional rounds, children might sort items into the baskets by other price ranges, such as "59¢ and Lower" and "60¢ and Higher." They might also sort by more than two price ranges.

Variations

- Have children sort the cards by three or more price ranges. Then help them show their results on a graph.
- Have children find the sum of the cost of two food items.

Egg-Carton Probability

Children use common items to explore probability.

Players: 2-4

Materials

- egg-carton probability recording sheet (page 43)
- egg carton
- blue and red dot stickers (six of each color)
- penny
- wipe-off marker
- paper towels

Getting Ready

1. Open the egg carton. Place a red or blue dot sticker in the bottom of each cup, alternating the colors in each row of cups.

2. Copy and laminate the egg-carton probability recording sheet.

How to Play

1. Place the penny in the egg carton. Close the lid.

2. The first player predicts whether the penny will land in a red or blue cup. He or she shakes the carton and opens the lid to check which color the penny landed on.

3. The player finds the corresponding egg on the recording sheet and marks off a box on that egg. (Players should mark the boxes in numerical order starting with 1 and ending with 20.)

4. Players take turns making predictions, shaking the penny in the egg carton, and recording their results. Play continues until all the boxes on the blue or red egg have been marked.

5. Discuss the results with children. Then use paper towels to erase the boxes on the eggs for the next round of play.

Variations

- Use more dot stickers of one color than the other color in the egg carton. For example, use eight blue stickers and four red stickers. Discuss the results after children complete the activity.
- Put a colored dot sticker in the bottom of one of the egg cups. Ask children to predict how many times they think the penny might land on the dot in 20 tries. After completing the activity, have them compare their predictions to the actual number.

Egg-Carton Probability
Recording Sheet

Blue

1	2	3	4	5
6	7	8	9	10
11	12	13	14	15
16	17	18	19	20

Red

1	2	3	4	5
6	7	8	9	10
11	12	13	14	15
16	17	18	19	20

Scoop-and-Estimate

Children estimate how many small objects it takes to fill a laundry detergent scoop.

Players: 2-3

Materials

- scoop-and-estimate recording sheet (page 45)
- 3 clean laundry detergent scoops
- 3 sets of small items such as dried beans, uncooked pasta shells, cereal rings, paper clips, and pennies
- 3 large foam cups
- wipe-off markers (one per player)
- paper towels

Getting Ready

1. Laminate three copies of the scoop-and-estimate recording sheet.

2. Write the name of each item to be used on a separate foam cup. Fill each cup with the corresponding item.

How to Play

1. Each player takes a laundry detergent scoop, recording sheet, and wipe-off marker.

2. Players draw each item in the cups and write its name on their recording sheets.

3. Each player fills his or her scoop with one of the items. The player estimates how many of that item are in the scoop. He or she writes the estimate on the recording sheet. Then the player counts the items in the scoop, writes the actual number, and compares it to his or her estimate.

4. Each player repeats step 3 for each item listed on his or her recording sheet.

Variations

- If children are using identical scoops and items in the activity, have them share and compare their results with one another.
- Help children create graphs to show their results.

Scoop-and-Estimate
Recording Sheet

Item	My Estimate	Actual Number
_____		
_____		
_____		

Data Collector Chart

Reinforce graphing skills with the data children collect in this pocket chart.

Players: whole class

Materials

- 8 letter-sized envelopes
- scissors
- posterboard
- glue
- craft knife (for teacher use only)
- index cards
- wipe-off marker
- paper towels

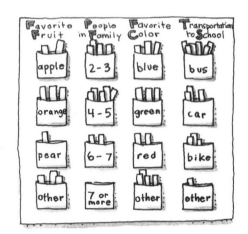

Getting Ready

1. Close, seal, and cut each envelope in half crosswise. Glue the envelopes (open ends up) to the posterboard to create four rows and columns. Leave extra space across the top to add column headings.

2. Laminate the chart. Use a craft knife to slit open the top edge of each envelope pocket.

3. Cut the index cards in half lengthwise to use as markers in the pockets.

4. Label one or more columns to show what kind of data children will collect (for example, "Favorite Fruit," "People in Family," "Favorite Color," and "School Transportation").

5. Write a choice related to the heading on each pocket in that column (for "People in Family," you might write "2–3," "4–5," "5–6," and "7 or more" on the pockets).

How to Play

1. Children read each column heading and the corresponding choices. They place a marker in the pocket that represents their choice.

2. After all the data has been collected, have children count the markers in each pocket. Write that number on the corresponding pocket and circle it.

3. Put the chart in a center. Send children to the center in pairs to create graphs using the data from the chart. Have the pairs share their completed graphs with others.

Variation

Have children write number comparison sentences using numbers shown on the pockets under a particular heading. Or have them make up and solve addition and subtraction problems with the numbers.

Tick-Tock Lid Clock

Children use clocks with moveable hands to practice telling time.

Players: 4

Materials

- analog clock patterns and digital clock cards (pages 48–49)
- crayons
- scissors
- craft glue
- four 6 ¼-inch plastic lids (from 3-lb. margarine tubs)
- 4 paper brads
- clear wide packing tape
- pair of dotted dice
- wipe-off markers (one per player)
- paper towels

Getting Ready

1. Make four copies of the analog clock patterns and one copy of the digital clock cards. Color each analog clock face a different color. Color each hour hand red and each minute hand blue. Laminate and cut out the patterns and cards.

2. Glue each analog clock face to the inside of a 6-inch lid.

3. Use a paper brad to attach an hour and minute hand to each clock. Tape the prongs securely in place against the back of the clock.

How to Play

1. Each player takes an analog clock, digital clock card, and wipe-off marker.

2. The first player rolls the dice and adds the dots. He or she sets the hour hand to that number on the clock. Then the player rolls again and sets the minute hand to that number.

3. The player tells the time on his or her analog clock and writes that time on the digital clock card. The other players check to make sure the times on both clocks agree.

4. Players take turns rolling the dice, setting their clocks, and naming and writing the time until each player has taken ten turns.

Variation

> After setting their analog clocks, ask children to sequence them from the earliest to latest times. Then ask them to tell how much time has elapsed between the times shown on two clocks in the sequence.

47

Analog Clock Patterns

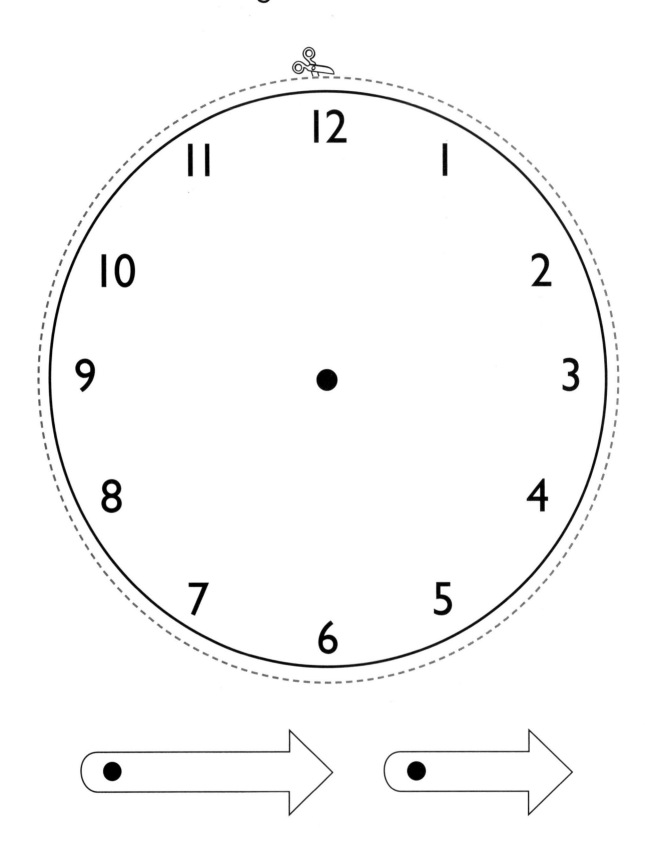

Digital Clock Cards

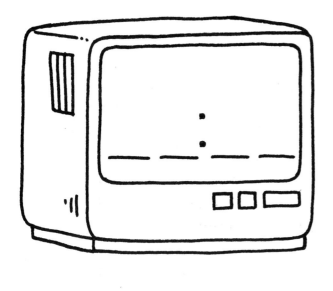
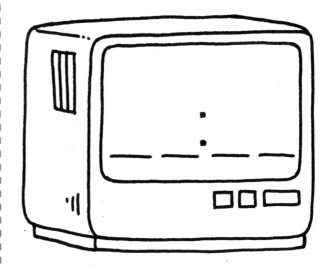
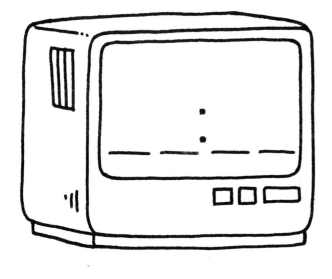
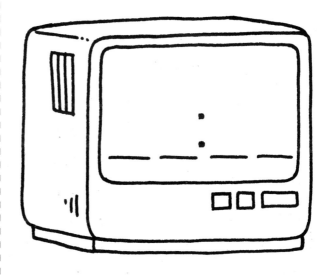

Money Bags

Children use these bag booklets to practice counting money.

Players: 2 or more

Materials

- money cards (pages 51–52)
- scissors
- resealable plastic sandwich bags
- department store sales flyers
- glue
- brown paper lunch bags (six per booklet)
- paper brads
- permanent marker
- hole punch

Getting Ready

1. Copy and color several copies of the money cards for each player. Laminate and cut apart the cards. Store each set in a separate resealable plastic bag.

2. Cut out pictures from the sales flyers to represent a variety of items, such as toys and clothes. Depending on children's money skills, you might want to set a limit on the item prices (such as $10.00). Cut out five pictures for every booklet you plan to make.

3. Glue each picture to a paper bag. Write the name of the item and its price.

4. Stack five bags together. Top the stack with a plain bag. Punch holes and poke two paper brads through the bottom end of the bags to create a booklet. Write "Money Bags" on the top bag. Number each book so children can tell them apart.

How to Play

1. Each player takes a set of money cards and booklet.

2. Players look at the item and price on each page. They count out the money needed to "buy" the item and place that amount inside the bag. Players buy as many items in their booklets as possible using the money allotted to them.

3. Players exchange booklets and check the money amount in each bag to make sure it equals the cost of the item on the page. Then they return the booklets to their owners.

Variation

Ask children to find the total cost of any two items in their bag booklets. Then have them count out that amount of money.

Money Cards

Money Cards

Inchworm Measurements

Children measure classroom items using this unusual inchworm ruler.

Players: 4-6

Materials

- inchworm ruler patterns (page 54)
- color markers
- scissors
- glue stick
- objects to measure (such as blocks, books, crayons, and paintbrushes)
- light-colored construction paper
- sticky note pads (one per player)
- pencils (one per player)

Getting Ready

1. Copy the patterns for six rulers. To give children a starting point for counting on each ruler, color the head circle one color and all the other circles another color. Cut out the patterns.

2. Glue the two pieces together to create one long strip. The inchworm's head and tail should be at the ends of the strip. Laminate the rulers for durability.

3. Gather six objects for children to measure. Choose objects that can be measured with one ruler length. Spread the objects out on a table.

4. Write a length-related question about each object on a sheet of construction paper. For example, for a book, you might write "How many circles tall is the book?" Place the paper near the object.

How to Play

1. Each player takes a ruler, sticky note pad, and pencil.

2. The player chooses an object on the table, reads the question on the paper, and uses his or her ruler to find the answer. The player writes his or her name and findings, in circle units, on a sticky note and sticks the note to the back of the question.

3. After measuring all the objects, players turn over each question page and compare the answers on the sticky notes to see if they agree.

Variation

Invite children to work together to measure larger classroom items, such as the length of a bookshelf or tabletop.

Inchworm
Ruler Patterns

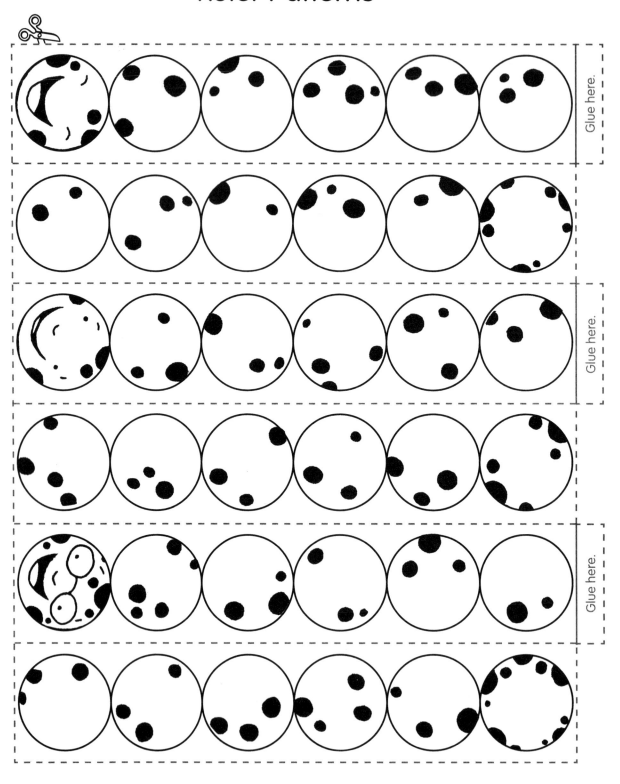

Temperature Zip

Children practice reading temperatures with a zipper thermometer.

Players: 2

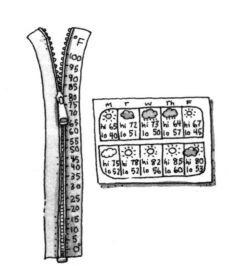

Materials

- two 22-inch zippers (light-colored metal zippers work best)
- ruler
- black ultra-fine-point permanent marker
- daily and 10-day weather forecasts (from local newspapers or weather Web sites)
- construction paper

Getting Ready

1. Beginning at the base of each zipper (not the zipper tape), use the marker and ruler to mark inch intervals along the right side of the zipper tape. Write 0° F next to the zipper base. Then write numbers in 5-degree increments up to 100° F next to the marks.

2. Mark four evenly spaced intervals between each inch mark to represent 1-degree increments.

3. Mount the weather forecasts on construction paper and laminate them for durability.

4. Write a temperature, such as 77° F on the board. Read the temperature to children. Explain that the small circle stands for "degrees" and the *F* stands for "Fahrenheit."

How to Play

1. Players choose a weather forecast. Each player takes a zipper thermometer.

2. Players zip their thermometer zipper to the first temperature shown on the forecast. They compare their thermometers to check their work.

3. Players continue zipping their thermometers to each temperature shown on the forecast and comparing their work.

Variation

Have children graph the high (or low) temperatures shown on a 10-day forecast.

Gallon Guy

Children explore liquid measurement with this helpful little guy.

Players: 2

Materials

- gallon pattern and liquid measurement cards (pages 58–59)
- crayons
- scissors
- 3-inch flesh-colored construction paper circle
- construction paper in various colors, including flesh tones
- glue stick
- yarn
- low-heat glue gun (for adult use only)
- plastic containers in the following sizes: 1 gallon, 2 half-gallons, 4 quarts, 8 pints, and 16 cups (make sure these are 8-ounce containers)
- plastic funnel
- water
- towels (for wiping up spills)

Getting Ready

1. Make one copy of the gallon pattern on page 58 and two copies of the liquid measurement cards on page 59.

2. Color and cut out the gallon pattern.

3. Cut out and group the cards by measurement units. Color each set of cards a different color.

4. To make a Gallon Guy, glue the 3-inch circle to the top of the gallon cutout. Then cut out arms, hands, legs, and feet from construction paper. Glue the pieces onto the gallon cutout, as shown on next page. Draw on facial features, but don't add hair in this step.

5. Laminate the Gallon Guy and cards.

6. Use the glue gun to attach yarn hair to the Gallon Guy's head. If desired, create a Gallon Gal instead.

How to Play

1. Children decide on a unit of measure to work with. They choose all the cards for this unit and fit them onto the Gallon Guy. For example, they might place the 16 cup cards on the Gallon Guy.

2. Children gather the number of containers corresponding to the cards on the Gallon Guy.

3. Fill the gallon jug with water. Then fill each of the containers with water from the jug as children observe. As each container is filled, they turn a unit card facedown on the Gallon Guy. When finished, all the selected containers should be filled with water and all the cards on the Gallon Guy turned facedown.

4. To check their work, children can count to make sure the number of filled containers matches the number of cards on the Gallon Guy.

Variations

- Have children use the cards and containers to explore the relationship of other units of liquid measurement. For example, they might fit pint cards onto a half-gallon card, fill a half-gallon jug with water, and then pour the contents into pint containers to see if the number of filled containers and pint cards match.

- Provide clean one-half gallon and quart-sized plastic containers, 1- and 2-liter plastic soda bottles, and cups. Have children predict whether the half-gallon or the 2-liter container holds the most liquid. Invite them to fill each container and then distribute the liquid into cups to find out. Have them repeat the activity using the quart-sized and 1-liter containers.

Gallon Pattern

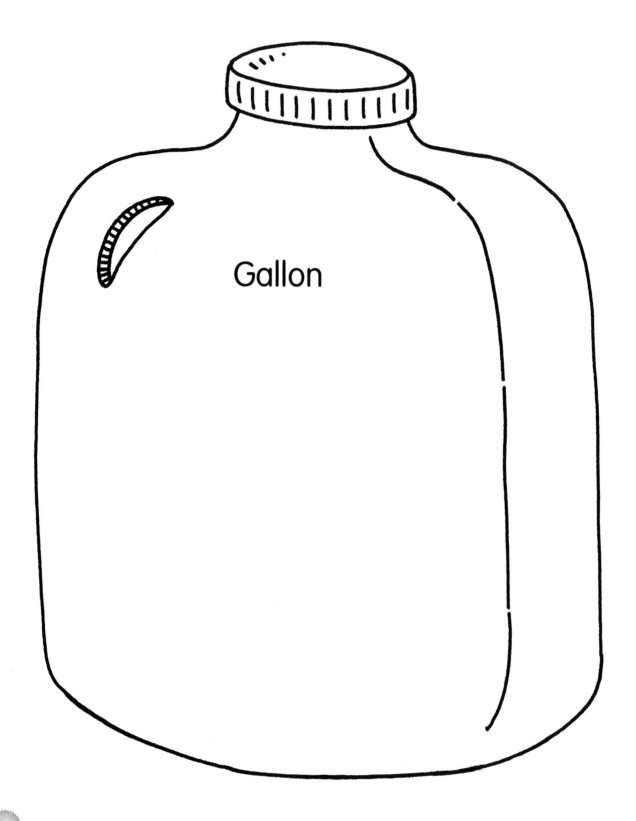

Gallon

Liquid Measurement Cards

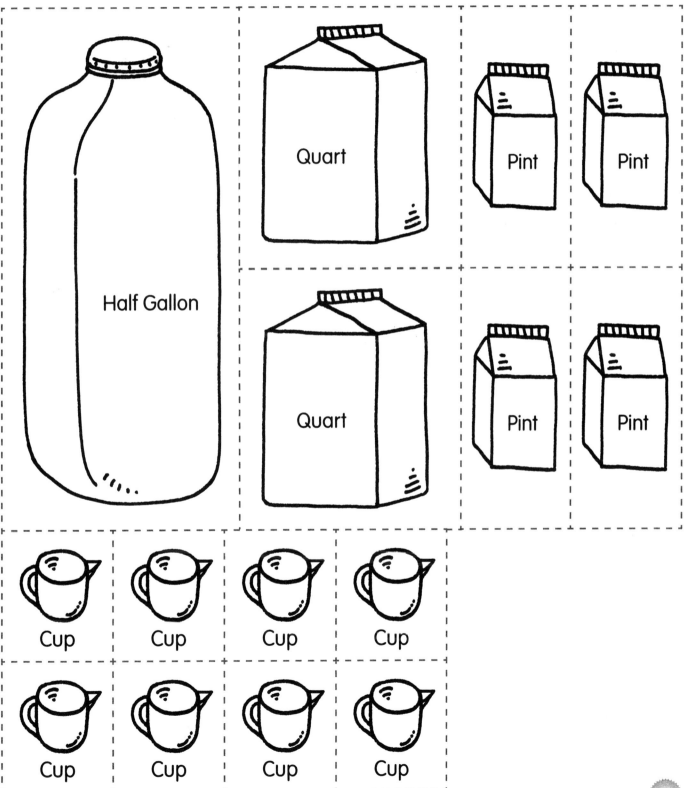

Word Problem Spin

Children solve a variety of word problems in this spin-the-wheel game.

Players: 2-4

Materials

- game spinner patterns and game cards (pages 61–64)
- crayons
- scissors
- tagboard
- index cards
- paper brad
- paper and pencil (per player)

Getting Ready

1. Copy the game spinner patterns and game cards. Color the sections on the spinner and the spinner arrow. Cut out the spinner patterns and cards.

2. Glue the spinner and arrow cutouts to tagboard. Trim the tagboard to fit.

3. Sort the cards by the symbols shown on them. Cut apart the problem and answer sections of each card. Glue the problem to one side of an index card and the answer to the other side.

4. Laminate the wheel, arrow, and game cards. Then attach the arrow to the spinner with the paper brad.

How to Play

1. Sort the cards by the symbols on them. Place each stack with the problems faceup.

2. The first player spins the wheel. He or she takes a card from the stack that matches the symbol the spinner lands on (if the stack is empty, the player spins again). The player reads the problem aloud, tells the answer, and checks the answer on the back. If correct, the player earns the points shown on the spinner.

3. Players take turns, writing all their earned points on paper. When all the cards have been used, each player totals his or her points. The player with the most points is the winner.

Variation

Prepare a set of game cards by labeling them with shapes, number problems, and their answers. Invite children to use the new set of cards to play the game.

Game Spinner Patterns

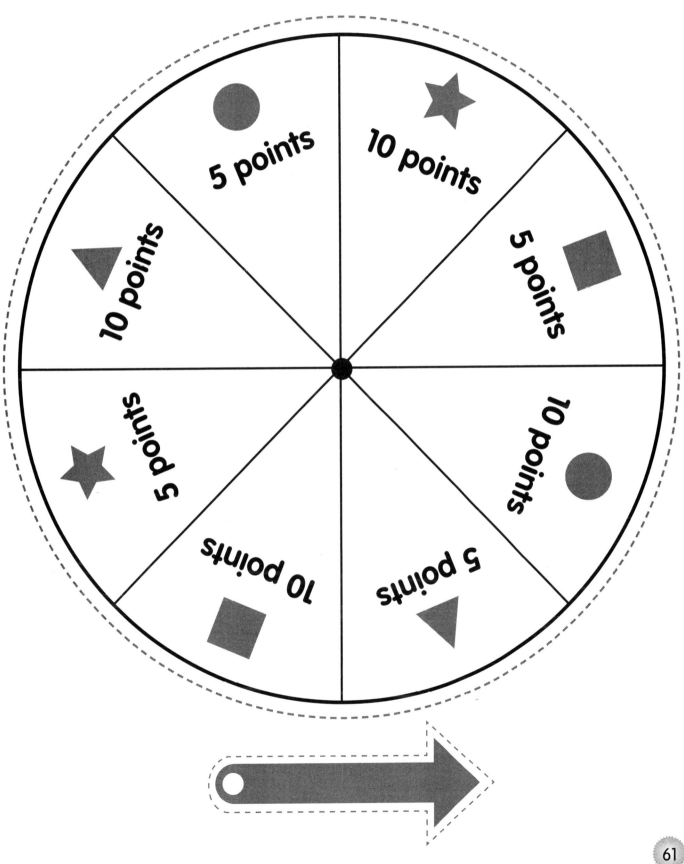

Game Cards

● Ana collected 47 cans for the food drive. Teri collected 39 cans. How many cans did they collect in all?

● Jim's class planted 72 flowers in the park. Ned's class planted 68 flowers. How many flowers were planted in all?

Ana and Teri collected 86 cans.

The classes planted 140 flowers.

● Meg picked 26 apples on Monday. She picked 19 apples on Tuesday. How many apples did she pick in all?

● George brought 21 crayons to class. Gina brought 18 crayons. How many crayons do they have in all?

Meg picked 45 apples.

George and Gina have 39 crayons.

● Vic made 8 craft butterflies. Pam made 9 butterflies. How many butterflies did they make all together?

● Sue read 32 pages in a book. Later, she read 24 more pages. How many pages did she read in all?

Vic and Pam made 17 butterflies.

Sue read 56 pages.

■ Juan is 7 years old and his dad is 35 years old. How many years younger is Juan than his dad?

■ Kylie brought 28 cookies to school. The class ate 19 cookies. How many cookies does Kylie have left?

Juan is 28 years younger than his dad.

Kylie has 9 cookies left.

Skill-Building Math Activities Kids Can't Resist! © 2007 by Michelle K. Ramsey, Scholastic Teaching Resources

Game Cards

Carlos had 15 lightning bugs in a jar. Six bugs flew away. How many lightning bugs are left in the jar?

Sumi built a tower with 31 blocks. Mary knocked over 8 blocks. How many blocks are in Sumi's tower?

Carlos has 9 bugs left.

Sumi has 23 blocks in her tower.

Calvin had 26 grapes in his lunch bag. He ate 15 grapes. How many grapes does Calvin have left?

Peg had 99 marbles. She lost 13 marbles. How many marbles does she have left?

Calvin has 11 grapes left.

Peg has 86 marbles left.

Mia bought a hot dog for $1.00 and a cookie for 35¢. How much did she spend?

Luis had $3.00. He bought a book for $1.75. How much money does he have left?

Mia spent $1.35.

Luis has $1.25 left.

Jan has two quarters and three dimes. How much money does she have?

Al bought a marker for 89¢. He gave the store clerk $1.00. How much change did he get back?

Jan has 80¢.

Al got 11¢ back.

Game Cards

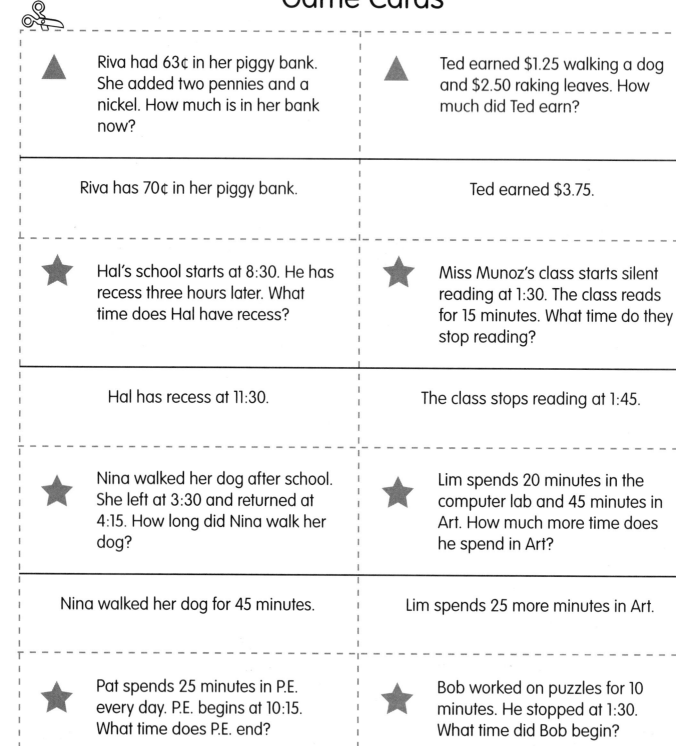

▲ Riva had 63¢ in her piggy bank. She added two pennies and a nickel. How much is in her bank now?

▲ Ted earned $1.25 walking a dog and $2.50 raking leaves. How much did Ted earn?

Riva has 70¢ in her piggy bank.

Ted earned $3.75.

★ Hal's school starts at 8:30. He has recess three hours later. What time does Hal have recess?

★ Miss Munoz's class starts silent reading at 1:30. The class reads for 15 minutes. What time do they stop reading?

Hal has recess at 11:30.

The class stops reading at 1:45.

★ Nina walked her dog after school. She left at 3:30 and returned at 4:15. How long did Nina walk her dog?

★ Lim spends 20 minutes in the computer lab and 45 minutes in Art. How much more time does he spend in Art?

Nina walked her dog for 45 minutes.

Lim spends 25 more minutes in Art.

★ Pat spends 25 minutes in P.E. every day. P.E. begins at 10:15. What time does P.E. end?

★ Bob worked on puzzles for 10 minutes. He stopped at 1:30. What time did Bob begin?

P.E. ends at 10:40.

Bob started working on puzzles at 1:20.

Skill-Building Math Activities Kids Can't Resist! © 2007 by Michelle K. Ramsey, Scholastic Teaching Resources